Earth

MW01204522

by Patricia Brinkman

Table of Contents

Introduction

Earth is a **planet**. Earth is different from all other planets. Earth has many living things. Read to learn about Earth.

Words to Know

 atmosphere

 axis

 core

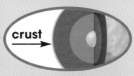 crust

 Earth

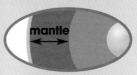 mantle

 orbits

 planet

 rotates

 solar system

See the Glossary on page 30.

What Is Earth?

Earth is a planet in the **solar system**. The solar system has nine planets.

Earth is the third planet from the sun. Earth is a sphere. Earth is the shape of a ball.

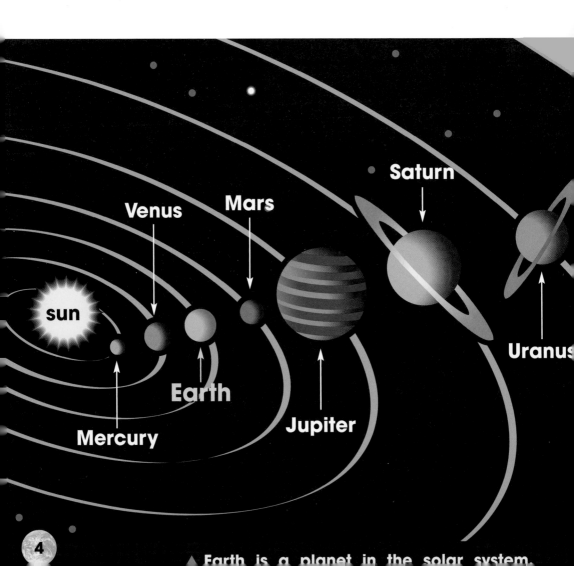

Venus

Mars

Saturn

sun

Earth

Mercury

Jupiter

Uranus

▲ Earth is a planet in the solar system.

Earth is the fifth largest planet. Four planets are larger than Earth. Four planets are smaller than Earth.

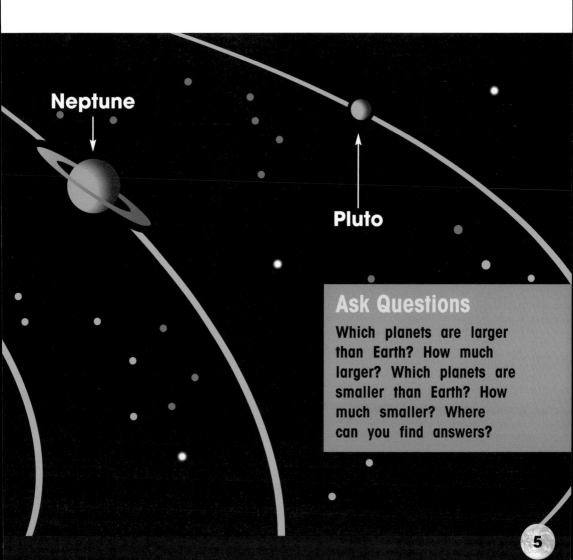

Neptune

Pluto

Ask Questions

Which planets are larger than Earth? How much larger? Which planets are smaller than Earth? How much smaller? Where can you find answers?

Earth is a planet that has layers. The **core** is one layer. The core is the center of Earth. The core is very hot.

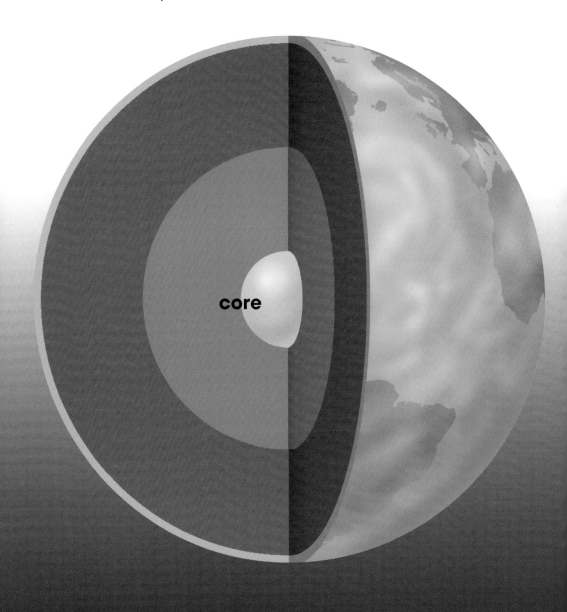

core

The core has two parts. The outer core is liquid metal. The inner core is solid metal.

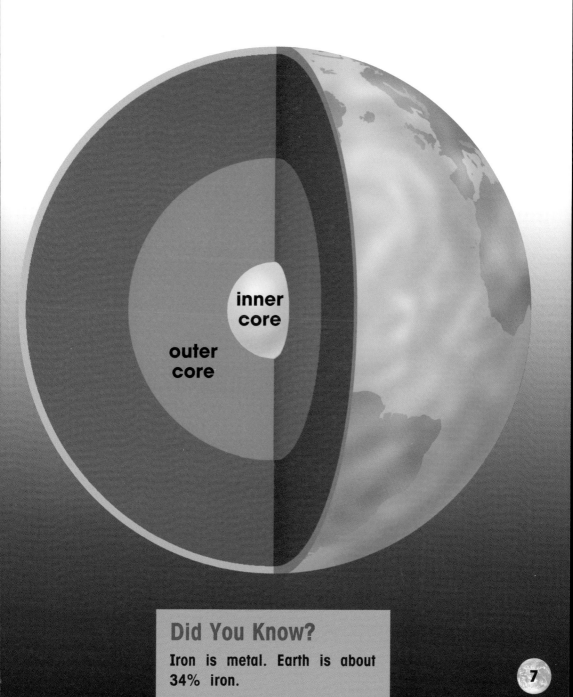

inner core

outer core

Did You Know?
Iron is metal. Earth is about 34% iron.

The **mantle** is around the core. The mantle is rock. The mantle is magma. Magma is hot liquid rock.

The mantle is very deep. The mantle is about 1,900 miles (3,000 kilometers) deep.

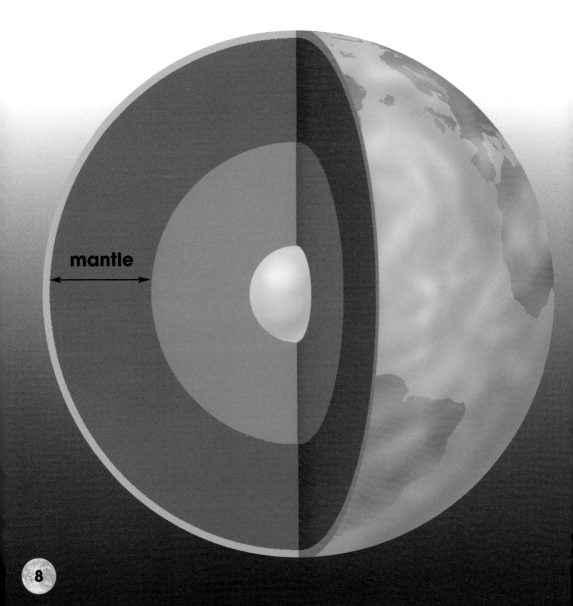

mantle

The top layer is the **crust**. The crust is mostly rock. The crust is the thinnest layer.

Earth's crust has many large pieces. The pieces are plates. The plates move.

crust

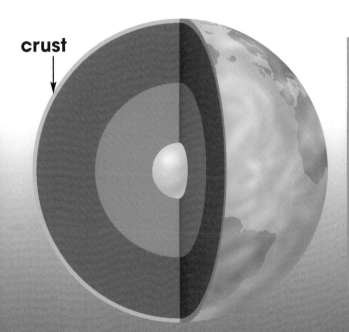

Try This

1. Take an apple.
2. Cut the apple in half.
3. The skin is like Earth's crust.
4. The soft part is like Earth's mantle.
5. The core of the apple is like Earth's core.

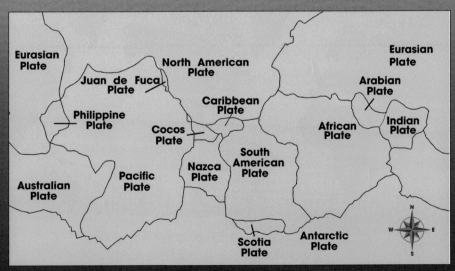

Eurasian Plate

Juan de Fuca Plate

North American Plate

Eurasian Plate

Arabian Plate

Philippine Plate

Caribbean Plate

Cocos Plate

African Plate

Indian Plate

Australian Plate

Pacific Plate

Nazca Plate

South American Plate

Scotia Plate

Antarctic Plate

N
W   E
S

9

▲ plates

What Does Earth Do?

Earth **orbits** the sun. Earth goes around the sun. Earth orbits the sun once every 365 days. One year on Earth is 365 days.

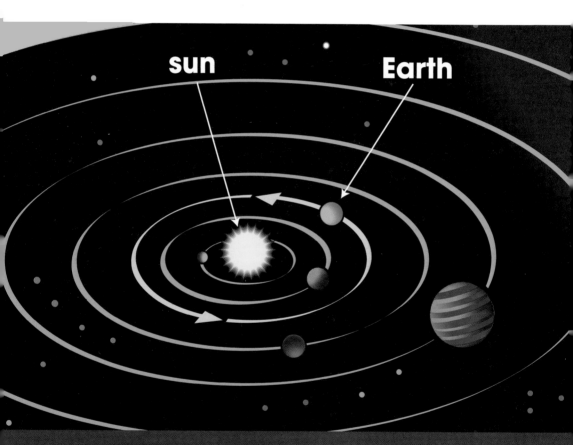

sun   Earth

△ Earth goes around the sun.

Did You Know?

Earth orbits the sun quickly. Earth travels about 67,000 miles (107,826 kilometers) per hour.

Earth has seasons. The seasons change as Earth orbits the sun. The seasons are:
- spring,
- summer,
- fall, and
- winter.

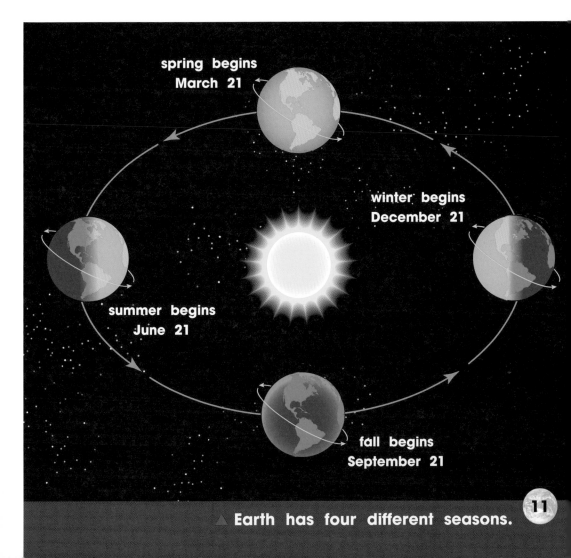

spring begins
March 21

winter begins
December 21

summer begins
June 21

fall begins
September 21

Earth has four different seasons.

Earth **rotates**. Earth spins around. Earth rotates once every twenty-four hours.

Earth has daytime because the planet rotates. Earth has nighttime because the planet rotates.

▲ **Earth has daytime and nighttime.**

Did You Know?

Earth has one moon. Some planets have many moons. Some planets have no moons.

Earth rotates on an **axis**. The axis is tilted. The axis goes through Earth. The axis is like an imaginary pole.

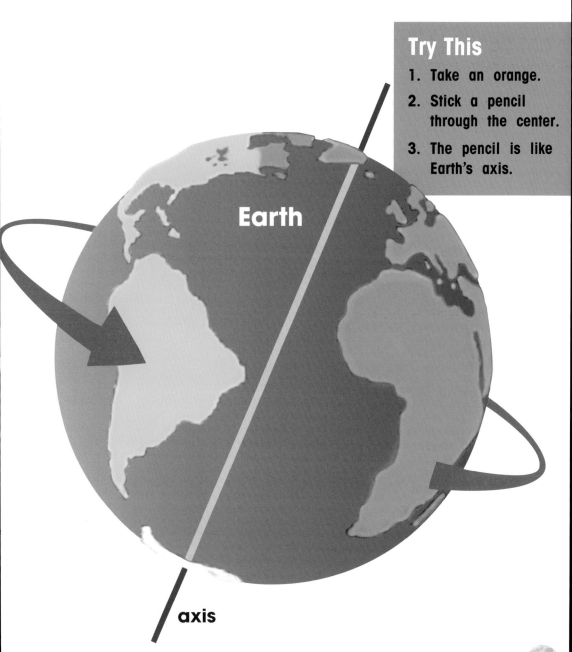

Earth

axis

Try This

1. Take an orange.
2. Stick a pencil through the center.
3. The pencil is like Earth's axis.

13

What Is on Earth?

Continents are on Earth. Continents are large pieces of land. Earth has seven continents.

Earth has different types of land. Continents have different types of land.

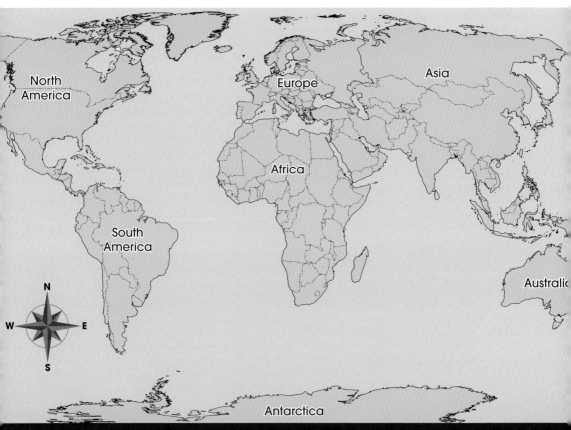

▲ **Continents are pieces of Earth's land.**

Mountains are on Earth. Every continent has mountains.

▲ **People see mountains on every continent.**

Deserts are on Earth. Deserts are mostly sand. Deserts are hot. Deserts are dry.

▲ **People find deserts on six continents.**

Rain forests are on Earth. Rain forests are warm. Rain forests have large amounts of rain.

▲ Many plants grow in rain forests.

Polar lands are on Earth. Ice covers polar lands. Polar lands are very cold.

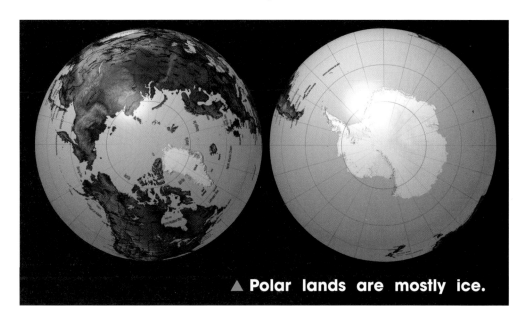

▲ **Polar lands are mostly ice.**

Grasslands are on Earth. People farm on grasslands. People raise animals on grasslands.

▲ **Grasslands are on many continents.**

17

Water is on Earth. Earth has four oceans. Oceans cover most of Earth's surface.

Earth has two types of water. Most water is salt water. Earth also has fresh water.

▲ **Water covers most of Earth.**

Did You Know?

Earth is the Blue Planet. People see photos of Earth. The photos show how Earth appears from space. Earth appears blue because of all the water.

Living things are on Earth. Earth's temperature makes life possible.

Earth is the perfect distance from the sun. Planets closer to the sun are too hot. Planets farther from the sun are too cold.

▲ **Earth has many types of life.**

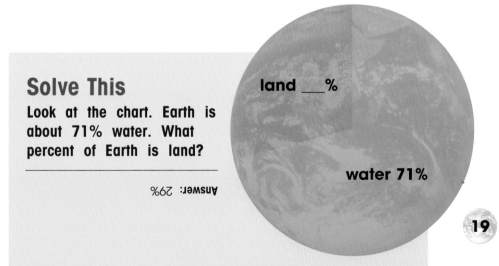

Solve This

Look at the chart. Earth is about 71% water. What percent of Earth is land?

land ___%

water 71%

Answer: 29%

19

Air is on Earth. Earth's **atmosphere** has air. The atmosphere is layers of air. The atmosphere has nitrogen and oxygen. Nitrogen and oxygen are gases.

Living things need oxygen.

Ask Questions

Why do living things need oxygen? Where can you find answers?

▲ Earth's atmosphere has gases.

The atmosphere also protects Earth. The atmosphere keeps heat during the night. It stops harmful rays from the sun.

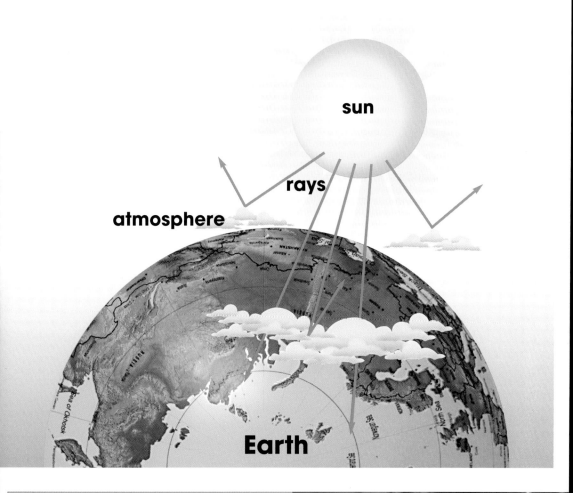

sun

rays

atmosphere

Earth

Did You Know?

Earth's atmosphere has three layers. The lower layer is where clouds form. The middle layer is about 50 miles (80 kilometers) high. The top layer protects Earth.

21

How Do People Change Earth?

Many people live on Earth. People cause many changes on Earth.

▲ **People live in many places.**

People use too many natural resources. Natural resources are in nature. People use Earth's natural resources too quickly.

▲ **People need natural resources to live.**

Earth changes when people clear land. People clear land to grow food. People clear land to build homes.

Did You Know?

People grow food in deserts. People pump water over long distances. They pump water to plants. Then, people use plants as food.

▲ **People work to clear land.**

People clear the land where animals live. Animals need to find new homes. Some animals can not find places to live. Some animals die.

▲ **People destroy the homes of animals.**

People change Earth by making Earth dirty. People put waste on Earth. The waste causes pollution.

Pollution hurts animals. Pollution hurts people. It hurts Earth.

▲ **Pollution changes Earth.**

Many people care about Earth. Many people work to stop pollution. They work to save animals.

Many people work to save Earth's natural resources.

▲ **People care about Earth.**

Summary

Earth has living things. Earth has three layers. It has different types of land. Many people cause Earth to change.

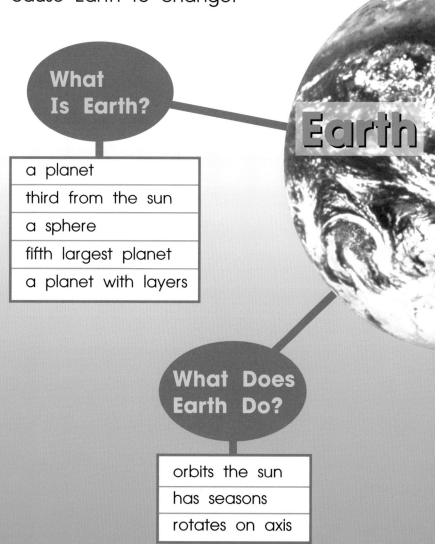

What Is Earth?

a planet
third from the sun
a sphere
fifth largest planet
a planet with layers

Earth

What Does Earth Do?

orbits the sun
has seasons
rotates on axis

What Is on Earth?

- continents
- mountains
- deserts
- rain forests
- polar lands
- grasslands
- water
- living things
- air
- atmosphere

How Do People Change Earth?

- use natural resources
- clear land
- take homes of animals
- cause pollution
- care about Earth

Think About It

1. What are some characteristics of Earth?
2. What are the different layers of Earth?
3. What are some ways people change Earth?

Glossary

atmosphere the layer of gases around Earth

*The **atmosphere** also protects Earth.*

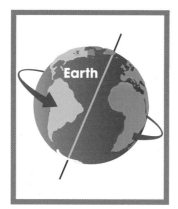

axis the imaginary line that goes through Earth

*Earth rotates on an **axis**.*

core the center part of Earth

*The **core** is the center of Earth.*

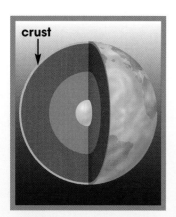

crust the outer layer of Earth

*Earth's **crust** has many large pieces.*

Earth the planet we live on

Earth is a planet.

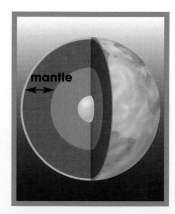

mantle part of Earth between the crust and core

*The **mantle** is rock.*

orbits goes around another object in a path

*Earth **orbits** the sun.*

planet an object in space that orbits the sun

*Earth is the fifth largest **planet**.*

rotates moves in a circle

*Earth **rotates** once every twenty-four hours.*

solar system the sun and the objects that orbit the sun

*The **solar system** has nine planets.*

Index